# The Way of Gratitude

## Fast Track to Enlightenment

By Rich Kenny

*The Way of Gratitude: Fast Track to Enlightenment*
(without The Gratitude Program)
is available as a Kindle ebook through Amazon

Copyright © 2012 Rich Kenny
All rights reserved.
ISBN: 978-1475108453
ISBN: 1475108451

# DEDICATION

To all people who know there must be a different way to live.

To all those who hope that what they have experienced of life so far is not all there is.

To all people who feel lost and yearn for something better and more fulfilling from life.

# Contents

| | | |
|---|---|---|
| CHAPTER 1: | GRATITUDE | 7 |
| CHAPTER 2: | HUMAN CONSCIOUSNESS ON THE RISE | 11 |
| CHAPTER 3: | PERSONAL GRATITUDE | 15 |
| CHAPTER 4: | EFFECTS OF GRATITUDE | 19 |
| CHAPTER 5: | WHO NEEDS GRATITUDE? | 23 |
| CHAPTER 6: | FIRST THINGS FIRST | 25 |
| CHAPTER 7: | ACCESSING GRATITUDE | 29 |
| CHAPTER 8: | TRANSFORMED BY GRATITUDE | 31 |
| CHAPTER 9: | TRAINING | 37 |
| CHAPTER 10: | GO SLOW TO GO FAST | 41 |
| CHAPTER 11: | ENLIGHTENED SELF-INTEREST | 45 |
| CHAPTER 12: | REASONS FOR GRATITUDE | 49 |
| CHAPTER 13: | RECREATE YOURSELF | 53 |
| CHAPTER 14: | APPRECIATION | 57 |
| CHAPTER 15: | A LIFE OF SERVICE TO MANKIND | 63 |
| THE GRATITUDE PROGRAM | | 65 |

# Chapter 1: GRATITUDE

*As each day comes to us refreshed and anew
so does my gratitude renew itself daily.
The breaking of the sun over the horizon
is my grateful heart dawning upon a blessed world.
—Terri Guillemets*

The word gratitude is generally understood to mean thankfulness, appreciation, or a kindly feeling for a favor received. In real gratitude work we take a deeper cut at the truth behind the word. Gratitude is more dimensional than what the words on this page indicate.

Gratitude is a powerful force. It can be described as a spirit or essence at the core of every person. If it is allowed to have its way, it changes lives. It has certainly changed mine. The emanation of gratitude changes the atmosphere around a person. People discover its magic in random moments when something happens to call it forth. But it is at your service constantly, like a genie in a bottle. Any definition of a spirit like gratitude is limited. We only know it when we experience it. It is possible to have the genie present every time we rub the lamp. We can do that consciously rather than waiting for a so-called good reason to bring him out.

For most people this is so simple that it completely eludes them. They may wish to have a different life experience, but they don't know how to go about getting one. It never occurs to them to simply be grateful. They imagine that the uncontrolled troop of little ducklings that make up their lives have to get put into a nice, neat row before they can make any serious attempt to transform themselves. Nothing could be further from the truth. Transform yourself and those little distracting ducklings come right around. Problems become opportunities.

Right with you, right now is one pure thing that could make all the difference. It is there for you. All you need to do is acknowledge it and accept its easy way. It is truly that simple.

The purpose of this book is to help you to make your acquaintance with gratitude and to point out the few basic elements of gratitude. Then, you can let gratitude work its transformative magic in your life.

It may seem like an exaggeration, but this may be the most important thing you will ever do. All the wonderful works and the creative endeavors to come, flow from this. Even if this was not true, you have nothing to lose in trying the Way of Gratitude. If it is true, there is a new, less tense, more joyful world ready for you to fill. It is charged with possibility and limitless horizons.

Try it and see how the things in your world can open up.

# Chapter 2: HUMAN CONSCIOUSNESS ON THE RISE

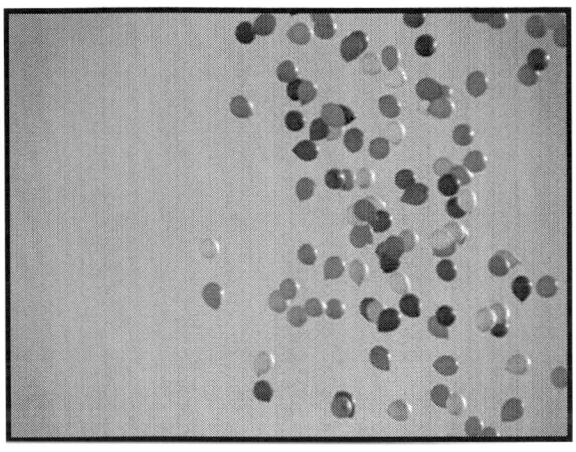

*If the only prayer you said in your whole life was, "thank you," that would suffice.*
−Meister Eckhart

Masked by the horrors in the world so doggedly reported in the media, there is something deeper and more significant happening today. A giant has been slumbering and is now astir. Human conscious is rising. It has been badly fractured and large segments of it are yet asleep. It is now being drawn forth again. For those who are tuned into the frequency of life, it is unmistakable. There are signs everywhere. From the drive for human rights and democracy to the ecology movement, people are awakening to a greater sense of fairness and their own responsibility for the world as a whole. Globalization of commerce and instant mass communication each can have a negative side, but they are also a means for the unification of human consciousness.

Everyone is experiencing the speeding up of life. Things are being created more rapidly than ever before. You get a new computer and in mere months, a new one with greater capabilities, is rolled out. Before long your new computer is all but obsolete, outpaced by advances in technology before you have even learned all that it can do. If you don't keep up with the constant upgrades, you get left behind in the pell-mell haste for the new and better.

There are new capabilities in the field of medicine, too. Replacing all sorts of human parts has become commonplace. Consider also how skilled and efficient we have become with tools of warfare. Today a button is pushed hundreds of miles away from its target and a missile whistles off with astonishing accuracy.

Social media has unified people in Syria, Egypt and Libya in their struggles for a more fair and democratic government. It helped to make the Occupy Movement a reality. It would not have been possible in the same way a mere decade ago. Certainly this is a sign of greater possibilities for the further unification of human consciousness. Much of what appears to be bad news contains within it the seed of the new and wonderful.

The fact is that however wonderful the capacities of humankind, they are no match for Mother Nature. Witness earthquakes in Haiti, Mexico and Japan. Floods everywhere, right along with droughts. A frightening nuclear power plant accident, with meltdowns, still simmers lethally in Japan. Hurricanes, tornadoes and tsunami are occurring with greater force and at a rate never before experienced in recorded history. Let's not forget terrorism, school shootings and crimes associated with drug wars and organized kidnapping. These are lamentable but they are also indications of humankind trying to shrug off the kind of life they should never have been living in the first place.

Diseases like AIDS and swine flu are modern plagues. The near economic collapse in the US and real financial collapse elsewhere threaten our accepted way of life. Evangelists will tell you that all of these are examples of the wrath of God. He is not happy. He is getting ready to bring hellfire and brimstone down on the inhabitants of Plant Earth. The end is near. It certainly seems like it some days. But there is no punishing God except in human belief. The true message is that we are not following the right way of life and that has consequences. Technological advances are not the answer.

If we remain at current course and speed, there is not much of a future for us. And what of a future for our children and grandchildren? Hysterical reporting in the media is a tremendous distraction, making it easy to miss good news. People are awakening to the fact they there is no answer in the usual approaches. There must be a better way. If they search, there are some things to be found. Things that point to an improved approach to living are rarely covered in the media and certainly even more rarely are they covered accurately.

There is scientific evidence that what people do and think matters. Organized groups of people meditating or chanting for peace have a real, measurable effect. That is, there are effects that are measurable. Who can say what more subtle effects occur that don't register on any meters, or how far they might extend?

What is your part in this rising of human consciousness? You may be inspired to join the meditators or chanters. Whatever you choose to do is fine. The most important and effective thing you can do to play your part in the great rising is to take hold of your own consciousness. Keep it in good working order. Don't let anyone else determine how you should be or how you should live your life - not the media, not religious or family traditions. You are responsible for how you live.

The most important tool I have seen for being responsible for myself is gratitude. It is the self-cleansing power for consciousness. I find that I cannot be both grateful and resentful at the same time. You can keep things that don't serve you out of your consciousness. Things that depress you, or distract you do not serve you. To support the awakening and unifying of human consciousness, choose a commitment to gratitude.

In this way, you play your part in the expansion of what is right and true and good. You join the unnamed movement that sends a silent message out in all directions: "There is a better way." For those stirring in their slumber, it is a gentle alarm clock. For those already awakened or awakening and beginning to search, it is a beacon. How satisfying to use a life once lost to participate in this great awakening.

# Chapter 3: PERSONAL GRATITUDE

*If you want to turn your life around, try thankfulness.
It will change your life mightily.*
—Gerald Good

Gratitude is personal. You do it alone. You do it for yourself. You do it for your own sake.

Gratitude is also impersonal. No one can claim exclusive right to gratitude. It will never be copyrighted or patented. Gratitude is free – freely available and free of charge.

Gratitude is for any person who desires it. It is universal. It is not limited by language or culture. It works in any geography. It works on land, at sea, in the air, under water, in space. Everywhere.

It is laden with rich gifts for you. No one can keep these away from you.

Gratitude is yours, freely given by life.

Gratitude is a living thing. It is a dynamic process. You start alone and discover who is with you in the river of gratitude.

The concept of sharing in a group, all with hearts lifted in gratitude is wonderful. However it is also fanciful and riddled with possibility of failure if you don't already know gratitude personally. You can catch a contact high, but you'll find that it won't carry into your every day experience for long. It is not truly sustainable, unless you, as an individual, are already familiar with the territory. Once you are, it is natural to attract others and to be attracted to others who share gratitude.

Like so much that is worthwhile, gratitude is a process. It requires focused attention while the process of gratitude builds momentum and a tiny seed planted at the outset of the gratitude journey sprouts and takes root. What works is to engage in the process without a timeline of expectation. Such an agenda will set you up for disappointment and possibly the abandonment of your project of self-recreation.

Processes like this one, need your patience and diligent engagement. There is nothing difficult about it. Our culture of consumerism has delivered the message that there is a quick fix for anything. Not so for this process. I am not saying that it needs to take a long time. Not at all. It doesn't take much, but it does take something – your commitment to it and your willingness to let it work at the rate determined by life, not by your expectations.

To be successful in your process, it absolutely requires that you take personal responsibility. How it goes for you is entirely up to you. No one can do this for you. You can't buy it off the shelf or online. Your commitment to see it through is critical. There will be early fruits, but don't settle for a snack when a feast awaits you. If you don't allow gratitude to move all the way into the core of your life, there is a real danger that you could settle for less and eventually allow the distractions of the world to displace it. If you settle or stop for any reason, even apparently good ones, you could develop the idea that you have done it all and never pick up where you left off. Discouragement can arise. This is actually a sign that you are making progress. You may be just a step away from breakthrough, even if it doesn't appear that way at the moment. What a shame it would be to quit too soon. Be alert to this.

Although those around you may notice changes, you are the only one who will know when you have done it thoroughly. How you know you have is when you can be thankful in any circumstance. As Krishnamurti said, "It doesn't matter what happens."

As unbelievable as this may sound to you now, it is possible. The point is that you can be thankful in all situations. It does not mean that you have to dig around for reasons to be thankful for any situation. I am not thankful for war, for child abuse, for all the suffering in the world, but I am still thankful. This makes all the difference in how I am in the world, no matter what.

You will learn to recognize an inner rising current that helps to lift not just your mood but also the atmosphere in which you live. This current is what you are going for in your gratitude process. When you can feel it, you have advanced to an important stage in your journey. All that remains is to lock it in as the way you engage with life in all circumstances. Is that possible? You bet.

Gratitude will move into your life, set up house and spread out comfortably. Your relaxed, assured present is contagious. Those who notice it will either be drawn to be close to you and the aura of your personal atmosphere or to be closed to you, because your presence reminds them of what they are not doing with their lives. That is not important. That is all about other people's choices. Let them have their experience. You may or may not have an opportunity to offer them advice about gratitude. Don't let it bother you if they don't get it. People move toward things like gratitude when they are ready.

You will likely feel closeness, even a greater sense of oneness, with those whom you connect with deeply in the field of gratitude. This presents a further possibility. A shared rising current can lift a lot more than a few people doing this work on their own. You can have a genuine experience of gratitude all on your own, like a hermit meditating on a mountaintop or in a cave, but what is of larger service to a waiting and needy world is to play a part in bringing the lift in a collective way. This is higher service, no matter whether it is acknowledged in the media or not. Secret service.

There is an amazing power when people are together in gratitude consistently. It can be contagious. It can go viral.

# Chapter 4: EFFECTS OF GRATITUDE

*You have given so much to me, give one thing more*
*– a grateful heart;*
*not thankful when it pleases me,*
*as if Your blessings had spare days,*
*but such a heart whose pulse may be Your praise.*
*–George Herbert*

Is your life working well for you? Is it working well in every area – job, home, relationships, family, the moments when you are alone with yourself? If you sincerely say that every thing in your life is okay and you feel on top of your life, you may not need to deepen your relationship with gratitude. However, if you struggle in relationships, if you worry about career, family or the state of the world, if you have a hard time coming to peace in yourself, if you often find yourself flailing in the swirl of all this, you can surely benefit from gratitude work.

Many people are plagued by their own emotions. Ever "go off" on someone? How about shrinking from speaking or acting even though you knew there was something for you to do? Have you ever been labeled conceited, remote or cold? How about aggressive and domineering? Too meek and mild? Do the most basic things sadden you inordinately? What do you really think of yourself? Are you a disappointment to anyone, even yourself? All that promise, all that wonderful potential, what became of it? Do you hold grudges? Do you tend to be a little bit judgmental at times? Ever feel stuck, like your life has dried up? I could go on but you get the idea. If you are plagued by disturbing emotions, gratitude can help. It is not a cure-all, but it can give you enough inner clarity to allow the power moving through your emotions to work for you and not against you.

The impulse to retreat from emotions is understandable, but it is not necessary. No doubt you have been hurt by deep feelings. Who hasn't? You probably have hurt loved ones with emotions that ran out of control. It may be difficult to express your feelings clearly in a constructive way without repeatedly venting the same old story. I bet your acquaintances get tired of it.

Change your story with gratitude and you change your experience. I once believed that I was the kind of guy who has trouble dealing with angry people. Now with the help of gratitude, I realize otherwise. People are people and their "stuff" is not mine. I see people differently and I can tell they are seeing me differently. People will see you differently with gratitude. More importantly, you will experience yourself differently.

There are a myriad of therapies and processes that you might benefit from and you should remain open to exploring them. Gratitude will not solve all your problems. It will give you fresh perspective on yourself and your circumstances. It will in no way interfere with any other work

– therapy, self-help, 12 step or other, that you choose to engage in. It will enhance it. I can attest to this by my own experience. Why not go for it? You've got nothing to lose except discomfort and miseries.

# Chapter 5: WHO NEEDS GRATITUDE?

*No duty is more urgent than that of returning thanks."*
*—Unknown*

There is no one who would not benefit from gratitude work. For those who have developed a level of mastery with gratitude, you already know this. In fact, you are probably not reading this book. The benefits are quite extensive. You will find them throughout the book.

If the possibility of recreating your life through this one thing seems too basic or simple, don't let that fool you. Gratitude is powerful in its elegant simplicity. No one can become adept at living a meaningful life and becoming a real blessing to others without knowing gratitude. If not for yourself, consider your family, friends, coworkers and neighbors. Isn't it better, more fun and even inspiring to be with a person who is relaxed and happy than with someone who is constantly griping, stressing, worrying aloud and depressive? Also, consider the world, which is clearly in need of help. You can quietly add to the possibilities for a better world by being thankful. Don't believe me? Just try it.

What can one person do? There is only one way to find out. As I introduce the possibilities for creative change for your life and for the world, I get excited. I'm pulling for you to engage in this work and go somewhere with it. Where you might go is not up to me, but I am certain it will be powerfully transformative.

The direct answer to the question of who is gratitude for is: it's for you.

## Chapter 6: FIRST THINGS FIRST

*Gratitude is riches. Complaint is poverty."*
*–Doris Day*

Let me be direct. There is no better time to do this work than the first thing upon rising. It sets an atmospheric tone for you and for your day. When the rising tide of gratitude becomes familiar, it will be natural to want to have that friend closely with you throughout your day. If it is put off there is a good chance that the interests and distractions of the day will displace the desire to connect in this way. "I can always get to this later." Don't bet on it. And I mean bet your life. If you are anything like me, that is, if you have a tendency to get a bit lazy in thinking, the needs and duties of the day will almost certainly displace your awareness of gratitude. Don't depend on finding the time and the consciousness of gratitude later. "First things first" is the rule.

This is especially so early in your journey into gratitude. You can become familiar and start to take it for granted. What happens to your other relationships when you take them for granted? You risk letting them fade. Doing that, you could lose a friend. You think you know someone and that you can rely on him or her when you need them. Meanwhile, you have changed and so have they. There is no guarantee of the permanence of any relationship. Don't take love for granted. You are developing a love relationship with gratitude. Respect yourself and your commitment enough to follow through even when you don't seem to have the time, energy or interest on the surface. It has been said that the one who thinks he doesn't have 30 minutes to meditate needs to meditate for an hour.

There will be times when you just don't feel like it, when you seem to have more important things to attend to. You tell yourself that a little skip won't make much of a difference. In fact a skip or two isn't all that terrible. The problem comes when you see that you can get along just fine without doing your gratitude work. In the short term that's most likely true. The more insidious problem is that there actually is just a tiny bit of unseen slippage in your commitment. If left unattended, the slippage continues subtly but with mounting momentum. Sooner or later, you drift away from gratitude like slipping away from any other friend. You lose track of it.

One day, you remember gratitude, probably when difficulties you experienced before engaging with gratitude come back to visit. It is said of someone entering rehab with a drug or alcohol addiction that his or her first time in rehab is the easiest to attain success. If the first time through doesn't stick, the chances of future success decline. To compare gratitude with addiction may seem misleading. Look at it this way. If you must have one addiction, let it be thankfulness.

If you fail to follow through, the voices inside your head that beat you up may start again, telling you, "You're no good at all. You never finish anything. You're weak." That won't assist you to get back on track. It's one more thing to overcome to complete your work. Don't risk it. On the other hand, should you have an interruption, a failing of some sort, pick yourself up. Don't beat yourself up. Gratitude will be waiting for you without an iota of judgment.

In short, there is no better time to do gratitude work than first thing in the morning. It starts the ball rolling on the rising, lifting tide called gratitude.

# Chapter 7: ACCESSING GRATITUDE

*In our daily lives,
we must see that it is* not happiness that makes us grateful,
but the gratefulness that makes us happy.
-Albert Clarke

It may be useful to set up your own sanctuary or special place to do your gratitude work, but it is absolutely unnecessary. At the outset of your gratitude journey it can definitely be helpful. Gratitude is always available, everywhere. Consider stories like those of Nelson Mandela, Victor Frankl and others who have suffered the limitations and indignities of unjust imprisonment. They emerged from their circumstances stronger, clearer and able to make a very positive contribution to mankind. They must have found a way to keep gratitude alive in their dire circumstances.

Most of us have it easier. That doesn't mean that we will all find gratitude. Some think that gratitude work means some kind of public display that they would find distasteful. That's not true. It is usually a quiet inner experience that affects your circumstance without any outer display at all. In that way, it is fair to call it secret service. There is at least one person who is not being whipped around unconsciously in reaction to what is occurring in their experience. That can make a huge difference. In your own experience, it makes whatever you experience more tolerable. It can also be a balm of relief for those who might be casting about like a drowning person in a sea of troubles to be in the presence of someone who is not.

So, gratitude, any time, anywhere. It might help to begin in a specially constructed cocoon for the butterfly of gratitude to grow strong and emerge in all its beauty. Let gratitude be protected so that it has a viable life. Then, where you do it will matter less and less.

I have created a daily practice of invoking my rising current of gratitude every morning. I walk with my dog, Pan, a truly adventurous White German Shepherd, and use the practice I developed over time to invoke gratitude. I am careful not to freak others out, but when it is reasonable, I use my voice to audibly express gratitude. This is not necessary, but I found it to be my way. Gratitude work is personal. Where and how you create connection with this creative force is entirely up to you. Please don't feel that you should imitate my experience or practice. No doubt there are as many ways to do this as there are people. Don't settle for the way anyone else has done it. You will find your own way if you stick to the program.

# Chapter 8: TRANSFORMED BY GRATITUDE

*The moment one gives close attention to anything,
even a blade of grass,
it becomes a mysterious, awesome, indescribably
magnificent world in itself."*
–Henry Miller

I am indebted to gratitude. It has totally transformed my life. There is no reason that you cannot transform your life. Here's how I stumbled upon gratitude and how it altered my experience.

As a one-time chef and current leader of a spiritual retreat center, there was a time when the difficulties I encountered in my day, dealing with everyday things, really troubled me. It might be assumed that someone leading a spiritual retreat center was above all that -coasting through his day, polishing his halo and chanting mantras. Not me. Although I know plenty of people who use mantras regularly and swear by them, I was never much for them. Just not my thing, I guess. Turns out that my thing is gratitude. I just hadn't cottoned to that notion yet.

I will spare you the mountain of ills that I had constructed from the molehills of my world. They are not gone away, but I am now able to maintain a workable perspective on them. I don't get swept off my pins any more.

Early one morning, just after dawn I was walking our previous dog, the good Domino. God rest his Dalmatian soul. I was completely missing the spectacular sunrise, the gardens in bloom and the sky filled with birdsong. I was gnawing away on the problems of the day. Things I do and decisions I make affect others, most of them friends. I was using my early morning time to worry uselessly. My mother always told me that worrying doesn't do any good. Not that she was much of an example. She worried constantly.

This would be the morning that I would not only find out how right she was, but also I would also find something that would eventually displace worry from my life thoroughly.

I trudged on dutifully in my usual way tossing around my problems around the way Domino ragged around his toys. We go out because Domino needs his exercise and to do his business. I just need my exercise.

Nothing seemed particularly special about that morning. Nothing to herald how it would impact my experience. There were no premonitions, no special signs in the heavens or trumpeting cherubs announcing what was in the offing.

After a frustrating while, I was ready to give it all up, but I didn't know how. I considered leaving my position, and my friends to try something else. The only reason I didn't was that I sensed that my habit of worrying would follow me, track me down and pounce again. What was the use?

That's when I looked up and saw the sky, aflame with a glorious sunrise. The brilliant greens of avocado and orange groves surrounded me. The birds were erupting in song on all sides for no better reason than to praise the day. Without thinking, I joined them. I'm no American Idol, but I have always loved to sing in the shower, the car, when I'm cooking. Suddenly, song just poured out of me. It was remarkable, and surprising.

I generally wince at the thought of hymns ~ too churchy. Dinosaurs of bygone times to me. I didn't have any use for them. So it astonished me that it was a hymn that came pouring out of me. I was startled. I was embarrassed ~ nearly overwhelmed. Being the only one around, I shrugged. I gave it full throat.

After a few moments, I came to my senses and stopped. What would people say? What if the neighbors heard? All I had discovered was something else to worry over. Then it hit me. For those few moments, I had been relieved of my troubles. Hot damn. That was cool.

I returned home with Domino and got busy about my day. Soon the experience was forgotten. The next morning on our walk, I remembered what had happened the prior morning. It couldn't be, could it? Could lightning strike twice? I had no audience and nothing to lose, so I tried it again. Same song too. One I'd never have imagined would do anything for me but mild nausea. Immediately there it was, relief from the slings and arrows of outrageous fortune.

I may not be the smartest guy you'll ever meet, but I will use what works and this worked. Amazing. I began to use that same hymn every morning. This went on for a few weeks during which I felt the steadying effect that my singing brought persist longer into my day. I eventually experimented, purposely not singing one or two mornings. The difference was enough to convince me. Something mysterious, even magical was at work here, but what is it?

I started to pay close attention. I noticed something that seemed to rise like a column of water within me during my early morning singing – a waterfall in reverse, cascading upwards with growing force. Sing the song and whoosh, there it would be. I liked it, a lot. The rising current elated me for a while. How lovely. How magical.

It was so strong; I could cling to it like a life raft. When I recalled it during the day, its effect appeared then as well. Whenever I remembered it, no matter how dense and heavy my circumstance, I felt its lift. I was clearly onto something and had enough sense to stay with it. I made it my primary and most important practice. Every morning, no matter what, I was out walking in the morning singing.

Over time, the force of the rising current kept growing. I could invoke it in an instant and at will. The current was changing as well. Instead of rising water, it began to feel like a column of fire. How biblical! I realized that the fire could consume my troubles or burn them into manageable pieces. That was a new perspective for me. I now had a reliable tool that could give me real lift in any situation. I had an effective antidote for things that would really shake me before.

I don't remember how long it took to put a name to this current. One day I just knew it was gratitude. My stuck life was being transformed by gratitude. Eventually I realized that gratitude wasn't just for me, it was me. It wasn't coming from outside of me and I didn't create it. This was a significant insight – I understood that gratitude is part of my nature. If there was a specific moment when I understood gratitude, this was it.

No need to be embarrassed by my own nature. I am proudly grateful beyond the words, the hymn or the practice. The singing helped me to realize it. I am gratitude. That changes everything.

I can share a few things now, after being involved with my gratitude practice for several years. It is easy. It is reliable. It costs nothing but a little time. Gratitude is the anti-venom for resentment. I cannot be both grateful and resentful at the same time. Resentment, if it takes root and is allowed to grow, becomes a dense, dark, unfriendly place. Resentments morph into judgments. Judgments cloud vision and obscure the beauty and peace of the moment. Given time and the least bit of energy, judgments ferment and breed toxins. They ruin friendships. They keep a person small and self-concerned. That is no way to live. With gratitude, I am able to create a space for clear non-reactive thinking.

I have established gratitude in a primary place at the core of my existence. This has changed everything. It doesn't matter if I feel I have been snubbed or treated unfairly. It doesn't matter that at times I cannot make both ends of my finances meet. It doesn't even matter if I am subject to others' judgments.

The comforting, empowering voice of gratitude is always with me, saying, "All is well."

# Chapter 9: TRAINING

*As we express our gratitude, we must never forget
that the highest appreciation is not to utter words, but to live by
them.*
–John Fitzgerald Kennedy

Discipline can be such a tough word. It evokes the image of a strict teacher bearing down with a punishing glare, like a drill sergeant. You make one small misstep and you get clobbered. No wonder is has become a dirty word to many people. They miss the point. Discipline is the tool to take control of our lives, to make ourselves productive and meaningful rather than aimless and shallow.

To train a puppy, you need to instill discipline. Otherwise you wind up with chewed slippers, stained carpets and a wild beast tearing up your yard and everything under your roof. Discipline will give you a happier pet. The puppy will know what is okay and what isn't. These days we call such things boundaries. What makes the difference for puppies is when discipline is offered in love. In fact, discipline is a dimension of love. You want to give a puppy everything it needs – companionship, food, water, shelter, exercise, etc. because of your love. You give your puppy the discipline of training because you love the little rascal

Our human capacities – our bodies, minds and feelings, are just like puppies. They are immensely enjoyable if they are not out of control. Out of control, they create havoc, don't they? You don't need a list of them. I'm sure you can make your own.

Why not treat yourself with the same consideration that you would give to your puppy? Your body and mind will respond in much the same manner. They will feel loved and know that they are cared for. Someone is looking out for their best interests. And who would know better the best interests of the various parts of you than you? Dedicated exercisers know this and they enjoy having an obedient, responsive body. Of course, exercise can be overdone when people assume the role of punishing overseer. I'm talking about real, unconditional love. Don't beat yourself up for failures, but lovingly insist that your body, mind and feelings do as you see fit. It's not impossible.

Discipline is important to gratitude work. It will not work on its own. It requires your thoughtful, loving guidance. There will be things that could interrupt your gratitude work if you let them. It is up to you to not let them. Following any kind of program will have challenges. Handling such challenges is your most critical function in befriending gratitude fully.

Assume an attitude that you will prevail, no matter what. Don't let anything stop you. Some things in your life are going to feel like life or death situations. Deal with them as you will. The "little foxes" that spoil things for you are subtle. Early success can be one of these. You could be tempted to let your alertness slip. Skip a day and not much happens, but the next day gets just a little bit harder to remember gratitude. It's all going so well, after all. If you let your guard down, it can be a slow slide. Then when a big impediment arises, you are not ready to handle it in the natural flow of life, in the easy current of gratitude.

Be smart. Be loving. Use self-discipline, to ensure your successful arrival at your journey's destination.

# Chapter 10: GO SLOW TO GO FAST

*Gratitude is a quality similar to electricity:
it must be produced and discharged
and used up in order to exist at all.
—William Faulkner*

Discipline isn't the only thing you'll need to reach the heightened state that gratitude offers. You will also need patience. Bear in mind that getting to that place within where gratitude reveals all its gifts is a process. Processes have their own pace, which cannot be predicted. It will come to completion if you stay with it. Discipline will keep you at it. Discouragement, if not overcome, will thwart you.

Let the process work. There is nothing much you can do to make it go faster.

That may not be what you want, but you must deal with it to complete your journey. The longest journey begins with a single step, after all.

Once you take that first step, impatience can make the destination appear to be impossibly remote. Keep going anyway. In a culture of instant gratification and quick fixes, there is an urge to get on with it. You may wish for a short cut. This is a seed of discouragement. The key to success is let the process move at its own pace

In the beginning you need to be satisfied just to be doing the work even if there is no measurable success. How can you tell if you are doing it right? Are you just wasting time? You're not if you stay with it. You must learn to trust the process.

I have a friend who leads mediation and consensus sessions. He is fond of using the maddening phrase, "Go slow to go fast." The first time I heard him use it; it made no sense to me. I could see what needed to happen in the meeting. If people would only give in to logic, the way to go was clear and simple. Eventually, I learned that until people are ready to move, they don't move with resolve all the way through to success. They may go along with the most vocal ones just to be relieved of the agonizingly slow process, but they won't necessarily buy into what the group comes to. Sooner or later, that kind of agreement crumbles and matters just get worse.

That same phrase can be applied to a process like the discovery of a personal relationship with gratitude. It requires patience, most of all. Patience is not a strong suit for many people in our "get it done now" culture. If you are patient, the rewards will appear in their own good time. You can't hurry love and you can't rush a process like this one.

There may be some early benefits for you. I trust so. However, they are the low hanging fruit compared to a full harvest of what gratitude has in store for you. Don't settle for less than the fullness of what life holds for you. You may be better off than you were, but you won't reach the status of one who truly steps into the noble position of serving the world with your gratitude.

Momentum will build. Patiently stay with what you commit to.

# Chapter 11: ENLIGHTENED SELF-INTEREST

*You simply will not be the same person two months from now
after consciously giving thanks each day
for the abundance that exists in your life.
And you will have set in motion an ancient spiritual law:
the more you have and are grateful for, the more will be given you."
–Sarah Ban Breathnach*

There are plenty of reasons to accept gratitude practice as a worthwhile and even critically important part of your life. Those of us who are attempting to lead a spiritual life or at least to be a good person may have to overcome the feeling that doing something good for you is not okay and is completely self-centered.

Of course we are good citizens. We recycle. We do nice things for others. We meditate, pray and give to worthy causes. There are so many needs in the world. Doing something that seems self-serving can be a challenge. There are so many people suffering in the world, how can I do something just for myself? Don't let that attitude stop you.

I have had an ongoing problem with self-care. I can do things for anyone else, giving of my time selflessly. Mentoring, coaching, teaching and advising do occupy a lot of my time these days. There seems to always be one more person that needs my time. I ask myself: "Do I have anything worthwhile to offer if I am not in balance in my own life?" I might have something to give, but it would be limited if I do not do everything I can to put myself in place to be of real service to others.

That makes doing gratitude work an act of enlightened self-interest. Sure, you commit time to making life better for yourself, but what's wrong with that? Plenty of people these days visit spas, get massages, take drugs or alcohol or disappear in the tsunami of media choices available today in an attempt to cope with the stresses of life in the third millennium of the modern era. Gratitude work gives a person exactly what others are spending their precious time and money to get with more reliable results.

If you commit to gratitude, you will get relief from stress, greater perspective on your own life and the most valuable commodity in the world, according to author Tom Robbins ~ freedom. Freedom from the smallness of self-concern.

Once you "get over yourself", you find a new world opening to you. It is full of the possibility of making a difference for others and therefore to the world at large. So, it is not self-concern after all. You can offer the wisdom innate in you that isn't blocked by playing small: "Who me?" You will find renewed energy to pour yourself joyfully into whatever is at hand – washing the dishes, providing useful insight to a friend, preparing a meal, walking the dog. You get over your pretense of smallness and you have the opportunity to fully step into your life.

This is a significant step for you and the feeling you once had of being important and making your contribution to the world is fulfilled. Is that really self serving? Of course it isn't. You are finding your way in the world. You are on the path you were born to walk. Step into gratitude work and make a difference in the world.

# Chapter 12: REASONS FOR GRATITUDE

*Saying thank you is more than good manners.*
*It is good spirituality.*
*−Alfred Painte*

For those who need more reasons to do gratitude work, here are a few.

Stress is a big issue for people today. The pace of life and the rate of unexpected changes keeps picking up. There are all sorts of methods people have adopted for dealing with stress. Some try to ignore it. They soldier on bravely (if not wisely). Denial has never done anyone any good.

Some take on habits of dealing with stress without realizing that that is what they are doing. Smoking, drinking, taking drugs, shopping, overworking (that's a good one for dealing with stress!), and receiving therapies of various kind - bodywork, etc., losing themselves in TV, videos games or surfing the net. There is some benefit in some of them, but they can be costly. Gratitude offers all the benefits of stress relief that people seek in these other modalities without the negative impact. I have had issues with elevated blood pressure. I have checked how expressing gratitude affects it. It helps a good deal.

Depression is a modern epidemic. Billions are spent for treatments and drugs to lessen its impact. But it hasn't gone away, it's still rampant. School children are being medicated for it like never before. It's a sign of the times, the curse of modern civilization. Gratitude helps. I can attest to that. Is it a cure-all? Maybe not, but it helps to ease the physical impact of stress. I don't recommend that anyone stop any treatments or program they are currently using. But, adding a gratitude program will not make matters worse and it may assist you to come to the point where treatments and drugs are no longer necessary. This is not a guarantee, but it is a possibility.

Gratitude is also ecologically clean. It generates no toxic residues. It involves no harmful additives, calories or anything artificial. Genuine and pure.

Gratitude is imminently cost effective. There is no gym to join or pyramid plan to join and pay for. There are no classes or armloads of books to buy. You simply do it at no cost.

One last reason for the thankful approach to living is that gratitude work is not limited by time or circumstance. Once you get the hang of it, it can be done in the office, on a bus, in a crowded airport, anywhere.

I heartily recommend it. It's like having the calming effect of a healthy meditation all the time. You don't need to reveal to anyone that you are engaged with gratitude.

Imagine a family holiday gathering – you know how stressful they can be, with one less stressed-out person in the mix. This is enlightened self-interest.

There is actually no reason not to do gratitude work.

## Chapter 13: RECREATE YOURSELF

*Life without thankfulness is devoid of love and passion.*
*Hope without thankfulness is lacking in fine perception.*
*Faith without thankfulness lacks strength and fortitude.*
*Every virtue divorced from thankfulness is maimed and limps along*
*the spiritual road.*
*–John Henry Jowett*

These days we get stories through the media of people who assume false identities in an attempt to get what they think they need by pretending to be someone else. Some are playing dangerous games on the Internet. Some have second, secret families. Some create fictitious biographies to enhance their image for financial reasons or career advancement. This is all based on a desire to have a different experience; one which they feel has been denied them in the limited conditions of their life. How sad.

What they are looking for they already have. It is buried beneath the worry and stress of living a life that is not fulfilling. I don't believe they will ever find satisfaction being duplicitous. It's been said that you must have a very good memory to be a liar. How good must your memory be to construct an entire life based on mistruths?

It may be true that what your life is now and how you go about living it are not satisfying for you. That is no reason to succumb to living a lie. Something has to change but it is not in the form of things. It is more basic.

There is a great relief in finding the truth of your own nature. Your true nature is enough and more. You can make a difference in the world and have a more satisfying experience.

Try a gratitude practice. Too simple? I believe simplicity is a good sign. Life by its nature is not complicated. People have made it complex and confusing. It doesn't have to be like that. The appearance that life is a morass of wrongness is what is wrong. People are trapped by following out what is expected of them.

We get signals all the time. We need to be alert and we need to understand the truth of what we are receiving. There was a man who heard this message: "This isn't working. I need to get a new wife." The real message that life was sending was, "This isn't working. I need to get a new life." If he acted on the misunderstood impulse, he would have further messed up his life. He is capable of recreating his life with the woman he has always loved.

The simplest and most accurate way to get a new life is to accept the simple power of gratitude. Who you are and how you live is no longer based in something that is a distortion of what life is telling you. It gets more and more accurate. It's possible that a man may need to leave his wife. It happens. But when it is done in unconscious reaction to unpleasant experiences, it is not likely to create improvement. It is likely to cause hurt and confusion. That won't create a better life for anybody.

What if the hypothetical wife in our example is only staying in the relationship to not cause hurt to her husband? What if she feels confined to her preconceived role? She may not be able to speak up without causing hurt. She may even take a lover just to force some play to be made. That is not the clearest way to create change. Of course, honesty is the best course, but there are factors that can make honesty difficult, especially when the people involved have begun in falsehood.

Take a breath. Start with a dedication to gratitude. The relationship may blossom anew. If not, a way will open that will be satisfying and victorious for everyone. It may include some grieving and there may still be some hurt, but not like what unconscious reaction creates. It is always better to be going towards something exciting that feels right and creative than to be fleeing from something you don't like.

Please understand me. I am not saying that fixing your relationship is valid justification for engaging in a gratitude practice. If it is what gets you started, so be it. It will eventually work out fine. It is all about gratitude.

If your life is not working for you now; if you are not satisfied; if you have a deep-seated sense that you have more to offer to the world; it is never only about the form of your life. You can reinvent yourself. Let life do the heavy lifting. Your best idea pales in comparison to what life has in store when you make yourself truly available. A dedicated gratitude practice will make you available to life. You can have a real life. Like Pinocchio, you may have longed to be a real person – one of value with something to contribute. Try gratitude. It is the fast track to enlightenment.

# Chapter 14: APPRECIATION

*There is not a more pleasing exercise of the mind than gratitude.
It is accompanied with such an inward satisfaction
that the duty is sufficiently rewarded by the performance.*
*–Joseph Addison*

It is natural to express appreciation for all sorts of things. Think about the ratio of appreciation to complaint you currently experience. If you are exceptional, it is 50-50, complaint to gratitude. Do you prefer to get appreciation or complaint?

Everyone likes to be appreciated. It is a rare person who enjoys hearing others' complaints, especially about them. Speaking your appreciation is a straightforward way to have gratitude alive in to your daily life. The sea never tires of sending wave after wave to the shore. That is its nature. Gratitude and the expression of it is a central part of your nature. Appreciate others regularly and you will discover an important part of your own nature.

There are ways to offer appreciation that are hollow and childish. Avoid these. Remember when you appreciate another person that it is all about them. It is not a chance to focus on your troubles or to inflate yourself for being magnanimous.

## THE FOUR S's

Here are guidelines I have for appreciation. I call them the 4 Ss. They are: Be specific, sincere, succinct and selfless.

**Be specific.** It is not effective to tell someone that you appreciate everything about him or her. Often someone receiving such a compliment gets confused or even suspicious. Can they trust such a comment? Can they believe it? They know themselves and their weaknesses and failings better than you do. It is likely to ring insincere. It could sound like this; "Mona, I really admire you so much. You do everything perfectly. You are always so bright and happy, etc. etc." Mona probably thinks, "How do you know that? Even I don't believe I'm all that. You must be up to something. Are you going to ask me a favor?" They are put on the alert, looking for the hook in the bait. You now have Mona watching you warily. The possibility for closeness has withered and a bit more distance has been introduced. Unfortunate. That is not the effect you want.

Try something like this instead; "Mona, your comment about the budget (or whatever) in this morning's meeting was sharp, clear and intelligent. Thank you."

Now Mona knows you have seen her. You paid attention and appreciated something real about her. She may have been thinking that her ideas had fallen on deaf ears. She may get discouraged and stop making the great comments. If she clams up, everybody misses what she has to offer. Something specific brings out the best in a person.

**Be sincere.** This one could go without saying, but in your enthusiasm, you could get carried away. Too much sounds hollow and weird. Then, if you offer an honest expression of appreciation, it may be too late. Once you've spoken without truth, you might not be believed about anything. Go for sincere every time.

There should be feeling in your appreciation and not just words. People innately trust real human emotion, but it won't help to go nuts over the boss' new tie. Tell him you admire his taste, but don't expect that will get you a raise. The opposite could even be true. He could sense a self-serving motivation in an insincere comment and that won't help you get that raise.

**Be succinct.** You really don't want to be a windbag when you appreciate. Being succinct indicates that you think about what you say. You are not just spewing. If you go on too long, you could appear to be out of control. This is good practice in any situation and especially so when offering appreciation. It indicates that you mean what you are saying, and are not merely speaking empty words.

Imagine someone bringing you this comment. "I just love the way you speak up at meetings, Mona. You are so brave. I could never do that. I'd be afraid of what people would think of me. I mean, what if I got it wrong? With all the big bosses there, you speak right up like it is the most natural thing. It's like you've been doing it all your life. I hope I have the guts to be like you someday. But I don't think I ever could. It's just amazing how you do that. I can't get over it. Did you learn that in your family or at school or what?"

I bet Mona stops listening early on. She will have questions about what this is. Is it really a compliment or a warning about speaking up in front of the bosses? Is it jealousy? It really isn't even about her. It's about the speaker.

It is much more powerful and effective to be brief. Try appreciating something that could have been captured on video - an action, some words, etc. "When you said..." "When you helped that little old lady across the street...." You can be confident that the recipient will know what you are referring to. That's a good start.

For a beautiful woman, a handsome man or good-looking child, they know they are attractive. They have heard it before, probably thousands of times. Try to appreciate something that reveals their inner nature, their true character. You will also avoid the insidious suspicious that you are really just hitting on them. Be clear and brief.

**Be selfless.** Being selfless will help you to be clear and avoid accusations of ulterior motives. Appreciation is about giving. There is nothing in it for you besides the opportunity to express your own giving nature.

People receiving appreciations often sense that someone is fishing for compliments for themselves. Don't go there. It often leads to a back and forth that stays shallow. A "who is best at being selfless" contest is ridiculous.

It's not a present you give and leave the price tag showing. There are absolutely no stings attached. Just give without being concerned for yourself.

Opportunities to give honest and healthy appreciation are always available. Don't become a maniac about it. Just engage and sharpen your skill as you go.

A final word on appreciation. When you are the recipient of appreciation the proper response is "Thank you." More gratitude. Resist the temptation to justify yourself or minimize yourself. "Who, little me?" That makes the person that appreciated you wrong and tells them the gift is not valued.

# Chapter 15: A LIFE OF SERVICE TO MANKIND

*Gratitude for the present moment
and the fullness of life now is the true prosperity.
–Eckhart Tolle*

Face it; the world's a mess. What can one person do to make it any better? With gratitude you *do* make a difference. It may seem infinitesimal, but it is something rather nothing. The world certainly doesn't need one more over-stressed, desperate struggling soul out to get more for himself. When you lift yourself above the travails of the common man, you make a difference. What do you think the world is more in need of  - more depression and avoidance or more happiness? The world doesn't owe you anything. You weren't born to be coddled by the world. Weren't you born for something nobler than that? You can begin to provide something to mankind in a simple way by accepting a commission of gratitude.

Those who discover the truth of themselves automatically remember the sense of service they were created with. Their living gives off a subtle, powerful signal - "There is another way to live." This is perceptible to those sensitized to it. People who have grown tired and discouraged can become sensitized. They want more from life. They may have experimented; distracting themselves from the unsatisfying life they have been leading. Some deal with personal dissatisfaction using drugs, alcohol, shopping sprees, eating like crazy, which is just that, crazy. They get further discouraged and either give up trying or redouble their efforts in their misguided pursuits. They need help. They need you.

Your presence can emit the sign they have been waiting for. I wonder who sent me that subtle signal when I unexpectedly discovered the power of gratitude. Waves of your emanation extend in all directions for who knows how far. Unlimited by geography or the laws of physics, they go out continuously as long as you keep gratitude alive. Your job is to make sure the waves are going out. They will have their effect. You may never know who has been touched or how it has helped them, but rest assured it has a positive impact.

There is nothing anyone can do to stop the message going out when you remain with gratitude. You can remain in gratitude no matter what. It has been done. Therefore, you can do it. This is the work of the common, everyday hero. This is the work you were meant to do. This brings hope to the hopeless. It finds the lost. All that matters is that someone does it. Aren't you someone?

# THE GRATITUDE PROGRAM

*Wake at dawn with a winged heart
and give thanks for another day of loving.*
–Kahil Gibral

    This self-directed program can easily guide you into an experience of all that gratitude can do for you. Step by simple step, you will open yourself to a force that is already existing in your own core nature. Take it lightly but seriously and its magic will work. You will experience more light in your consciousness, more ease with every circumstance and your eyes will open to opportunities to bring that light into the world.

    Throughout the gratitude program, you will only need a journal and pen. For those accustomed to doing most everything on a computer, please enjoy the physicality of handwork. It can be more immediate. There is a fresh page for each day.

    For your journaling sessions, find a comfortable, quiet place to work without distraction. It is best to have uninterrupted time.

    Relax, still your mind and go inside to where you can experience your most direct connection to the divine.

    Follow the instructions for the day with no hurrying or trying. Do your best to be in the flow of life through you.

Put your pen to the page and let *it* write rather than trying to get do the assignment right. There are no best or most correct answers. There is wisdom already within you that you access when you let it emerge without interference. Your good intentions and desire to "get it right" can interfere.

This is completely for you. No one else ever needs to see any of your writings.

*"Join me in the pure atmosphere of gratitude for life."*
*- Hafiz of Persia*

# GRATITUDE PROGRAM - WEEK 1

## THE SEED OF STILLNESS

Starting in stillness, we become familiar with the already present, rising current of gratitude, which we are each capable of but often neglect.

At the end of each day, as you prepare for sleep, write a list of 5 things that occurred during the day for which you feel sincere thanks. Anything, including the simplest of things, is fine.

Each morning compose a list of 10 things for which you are grateful generally. Do not repeat anything on this list all week. The simplest and the grandest things are fine.

Be alert for patterns that emerge in what you write but withhold judgment.

*Gratitude is a vaccine, an antitoxin, and an antiseptic.*
*–John Henry Jowett*

## WEEK 1 - DAY 1

5 things that occurred today, for which I am thankful:

1 -

2 -

3 -

4 -

5 -

10 things for which I am genuinely grateful in general:

1 -

2 -

3 -

4 -

5 -

6 -

7 -

8 -

9 -

10 -

## WEEK 1 - DAY 2

5 things that occurred today, for which I am thankful:

1 -

2 -

3 -

4 -

5 -

10 things for which I am genuinely grateful in general:

1 -

2 -

3 -

4 -

5 -

6 -

7 -

8 -

9 -

10 -

## WEEK 1 – DAY 3

5 things that occurred today, for which I am thankful:

1 -

2 -

3 -

4 -

5 -

10 things for which I am genuinely grateful in general:

1 -

2 -

3 -

4 -

5 -

6 -

7 -

8 -

9 -

## WEEK 1 – DAY 4

5 things that occurred today, for which I am thankful:

1 -

2 -

3 -

4 -

5 -

10 things for which I am genuinely grateful in general:

1 -

2 -

3 -

4 -

5 -

6 -

7 -

8 -

9 -

10 -

## WEEK 1 - DAY 5

5 things that occurred today, for which I am thankful:
1 -

2 -

3 -

4 -

5 -

10 things for which I am genuinely grateful in general:
1 -

2 -

3 -

4 -

5 -

6 -

7 -

8 -

9 -

10 -

## WEEK 1 – DAY 6

5 things that occurred today, for which I am thankful:

1 -

2 -

3 -

4 -

5 -

10 things for which I am genuinely grateful in general:

1 -

2 -

3 -

4 -

5 -

6 -

7 -

8 -

9 -

10 -

## WEEK 1 - DAY 7

5 things that occurred today, for which I am thankful:

1 -

2 -

3 -

4 -

5 -

10 things for which I am genuinely grateful in general:

1 -

2 -

3 -

4 -

5 -

6 -

7 -

8 -

9 -

10 -

Week 1 is now complete. We move on to Week 2.

# GRATITUDE PROGRAM - WEEK 2

## BEFRIENDING GRATITUDE
Gratitude grows more familiar

*Wake at dawn with a winged heart
and give thanks another day of loving.*
–Kahil Gibran

Contine the work of Week 1 exactly as directed.

Be alert to changes as gratitude becomes a part of your normal experience.

Gently note stuck places where it is challenging for you to be thankful. Just hold them in consciousness and let them be.

## WEEK 2- DAY 1

5 things that occurred today, for which I am thankful:
1 -

2 -

3 -
4 -

5 -

10 things for which I am genuinely grateful in general:
1 -

2 -

3 -

4 -

5 -

6 -

7 -

8 -

9 -

10 -

## WEEK 2- DAY 2

5 things that occurred today, for which I am thankful:

1 -

2 -

3 -

4 -

5 -

10 things for which I am genuinely grateful in general:

1 -

2 -

3 -

4 -

5 -

6 -

7 -

8 -

9 -

10 -

## WEEK 2- DAY 3

5 things that occurred today, for which I am thankful:

1 -

2 -

3 -

4 -

5 -

10 things for which I am genuinely grateful in general:

1 -

2 -

3 -

4 -

5 -

6 -

7 -

8 -

9 -

10 -

## WEEK 2- DAY 4

5 things that occurred today, for which I am thankful:

1 -

2 -

3 -

4 -

5 -

10 things for which I am genuinely grateful in general:

1 -

2 -

3 -

4 -

5 -

6 -

7 -

8 -

9 -

10 -

## WEEK 2- DAY 5

5 things that occurred today, for which I am thankful:

1 -

2 -

3 -

4 -

5 -

10 things for which I am genuinely grateful in general:

1 -

2 -

3 -

4 -

5 -

6 -

7 -

8 -

9 -

10 -

## WEEK 2- DAY 6

5 things that occurred today, for which I am thankful:

1 -

2 -

3 -

4 -

5 -

10 things for which I am genuinely grateful in general:

1 -

2 -

3 -

4 -

5 -

6 -

7 -

8 -

9 -

10 -

## WEEK 2- DAY 7

5 things that occurred today, for which I am thankful:

1 -

2 -

3 -

4 -

5 -

10 things for which I am genuinely grateful in general:

1 -

2 -

3 -

4 -

5 -

6 -

7 -

8 -

9 -

10 -

Week 2 is now complete. We move on to Week 3.

# GRATITUDE PROGRAM - WEEK 3

## BEING GRATEFUL FOR GRATITUDE

*Gratitude is the fairest blossom which springs from the soul.*
*—Henry Ward Beecher*

Continue all the work as you have begun.

Add into your journaling sessions at least three times each day when you notice the *absence* of gratitude.

As you pay more attention to gratitude and it increasingly becomes your experience, it is natural to begin to notice its absence. This is expected and actually a good thing. Just notice it and hold it in love.

## WEEK 3- DAY 1

5 things that occurred today, for which I am thankful:
1 -

2 -

3 -

4 -

5 -

10 things for which I am genuinely grateful in general:
1 -

2 -

3 -

4 -

5 -

6 -

7 -

8 -

9 -

10 -

3 times I noticed the absence of gratitude

1 -

2 -

3 -

## WEEK 3- DAY 2

5 things that occurred today, for which I am thankful:

1 -

2 -

3 -

4 -

5 -

10 things for which I am genuinely grateful in general:

1 -

2 -

3 -

4 -

5 -

6 -

7 -

8 -

9 -

10 -

3 times I noticed the absence of gratitude

1 -

2 -

3 -

## WEEK 3- DAY 3

5 things that occurred today, for which I am thankful:

1 -

2 -

3 -

4 -

5 -

10 things for which I am genuinely grateful in general:

1 -

2 -

3 -

4 -

5 -

6 -

7 -

8 -

9 -

10 -

3 times I noticed the absence of gratitude

1 -


2 -


3 -

## WEEK 3- DAY 4

5 things that occurred today, for which I am thankful:
1 -

2 -

3 -

4 -

5 -

10 things for which I am genuinely grateful in general:
1 -

2 -

3 -

4 -

5 -

6 -

7 -

8 -

9 -

10 -

3 times I noticed the absence of gratitude

1 -

2 -

3 -

## WEEK 3- DAY 5

5 things that occurred today, for which I am thankful:

1 -

2 -

3 -

4 -

5 -

10 things for which I am genuinely grateful in general:

1 -

2 -

3 -

4 -

5 -

6 -

7 -

8 -

9 -

10 -

3 times I noticed the absence of gratitude

1 -

2 -

3 -

## WEEK 3- DAY 6

5 things that occurred today, for which I am thankful:

1 -

2 -

3 -

4 -

5 -

10 things for which I am genuinely grateful in general:

1 -

2 -

3 -

4 -

5 -

6 -

7 -

8 -

9 -

10 -

3 times I noticed the absence of gratitude

1 -


2 -


3 -

## WEEK 3- DAY 7

5 things that occurred today, for which I am thankful:
1 -

2 -

3 -

4 -

5 -

10 things for which I am genuinely grateful in general:
1 -

2 -

3 -

4 -

5 -

6 -

7 -

8 -

9 -

10 -

3 times I noticed the absence of gratitude

1 -

2 -

3 -

Week 3 is now complete. We move on to Week 4.

# GRATITUDE PROGRAM - WEEK 4

## PERSONAL RESPONSIBILITY FOR GRATITUDE

*There is a calmness to a life lived in gratitude, a quiet joy.*
*—Ralph H. Blum*

Continue the work of the first three weeks.

Deliberately invoke gratitude as you begin each day.

Also, deliberately take gratitude into your every day life beyond your journaling sessions. Consciously invoke the rising current of gratitude several times each day by giving thanks in a way that is real for you.

Do something that is personal to you, outside of the journaling work. Sing a song of praise on a morning walk; enter into a meditative space devoted to gratitude or bring to mind impactful moments of your life when you were filled with gratitude, such as the birth of a child or discovering that someone who had been lost or in danger is safe, etc.

This is very personal. It need not be anything like anyone else's. Observe what this does in your heart.

Develop this as a personal practice.

Include a review of how you are doing with your personal gratitude practice in your evening journaling session. Also, review how deliberately invoking gratitude throughout your day went. Was it easy and natural to do? Did you remember to do it?

## WEEK 4- DAY 1

5 things that occurred today, for which I am thankful:

1 -

2 -

3 -

4 -

5 -

10 things for which I am genuinely grateful in general:

1 -

2 -

3 -

4 -

5 -

6 -

7 -

8 -

9 -

10 -

3 times I noticed the absence of gratitude

1 -

2 -

3 -

How my personal gratitude practice went today:

## WEEK 4- DAY 2

5 things that occurred today, for which I am thankful:

1 -

2 -

3 -

4 -

5 -

10 things for which I am genuinely grateful in general:

1 -

2 -

3 -

4 -

5 -

6 -

7 -

8 -

9 -

10 -

3 times I noticed the absence of gratitude

1 -

2 -

3 -


How my personal gratitude practice went today:

# WEEK 4- DAY 3

5 things that occurred today, for which I am thankful:

1 -

2 -

3 -

4 -

5 -

10 things for which I am genuinely grateful in general:

1 -

2 -

3 -

4 -

5 -

6 -

7 -

8 -

9 -

10 -

3 times I noticed the absence of gratitude

1 -


2 -


3 -



How my personal gratitude practice went today:

## WEEK 4- DAY 4

5 things that occurred today, for which I am thankful:

1 -

2 -

3 -

4 -

5 -

10 things for which I am genuinely grateful in general:

1 -

2 -

3 -

4 -

5 -

6 -

7 -

8 -

9 -

10 -

3 times I noticed the absence of gratitude

1 -

2 -

3 -

How my personal gratitude practice went today:

## WEEK 4- DAY 5

5 things that occurred today, for which I am thankful:

1 -

2 -

3 -

4 -

5 -

10 things for which I am genuinely grateful in general:

1 -

2 -

3 -

4 -

5 -

6 -

7 -

8 -

9 -

10 -

3 times I noticed the absence of gratitude

1 -

2 -

3 -


How my personal gratitude practice went today:

## WEEK 4- DAY 6

5 things that occurred today, for which I am thankful:

1 -

2 -

3 -

4 -

5 -

10 things for which I am genuinely grateful in general:

1 -

2 -

3 -

4 -

5 -

6 -

7 -

8 -

9 -

10 -

3 times I noticed the absence of gratitude

1 -

2 -

3 -

How my personal gratitude practice went today:

## WEEK 4- DAY 7

5 things that occurred today, for which I am thankful:

1 -

2 -

3 -

4 -

5 -

10 things for which I am genuinely grateful in general:

1 -

2 -

3 -

4 -

5 -

6 -

7 -

8 -

9 -

10 -

3 times I noticed the absence of gratitude

1 -

2 -

3 -


How my personal gratitude practice went today:

Week 4 is now complete. We move on to Week 5.

# GRATITUDE PROGRAM - WEEK 5

## PURIFICATION AND GRATITUDE

*Showing gratitude is one of the simplest
yet most powerful things humans can do for each other.
—Randy Pausch*

Continue all the work you have begun.

This week, pay specific attention to the times that are most likely to forget about giving thanks – stressful times, times when you feel too busy or too upset. What is it that distracts you? Perhaps there is some forgiveness work to be done of others or of yourself. This is an important part of your gratitude commission, to sanctify these things and integrate the emotions attached to them.

Work to be thankful, really thankful all the time. Don't settle for justifying lapses in trying circumstances. Anyone can do that. That's not who you are in truth.

## WEEK 5- DAY 1

5 things that occurred today, for which I am thankful:

1 -

2 -

3 -

4 -

5 -

10 things for which I am genuinely grateful in general:

1 -

2 -

3 -

4 -

5 -

6 -

7 -

8 -

9 -

10 -

3 times I noticed the absence of gratitude

1 -

2 -

3 -

How my personal gratitude practice went today:

Lapses and patterns of forgetting:

## WEEK 5- DAY 2

5 things that occurred today, for which I am thankful:
1 -

2 -

3 -

4 -

5 -

10 things for which I am genuinely grateful in general:
1 -

2 -

3 -

4 -

5 -

6 -

7 -

8 -

9 -

10 -

3 times I noticed the absence of gratitude

1 -

2 -

3 -

How my personal gratitude practice went today:

Lapses and patterns of forgetting:

## WEEK 5- DAY 3

5 things that occurred today, for which I am thankful:
1 -

2 -

3 -

4 -

5 -

10 things for which I am genuinely grateful in general:
1 -

2 -

3 -

4 -

5 -

6 -

7 -

8 -

9 -

10 -

3 times I noticed the absence of gratitude

1 -

2 -

3 -

How my personal gratitude practice went today:

Lapses and patterns of forgetting:

## WEEK 5- DAY 4

5 things that occurred today, for which I am thankful:
1 -

2 -

3 -

4 -

5 -

10 things for which I am genuinely grateful in general:
1 -

2 -

3 -

4 -

5 -

6 -

7 -

8 -

9 -

10 -

3 times I noticed the absence of gratitude

1 -

2 -

3 -

How my personal gratitude practice went today:

Lapses and patterns of forgetting:

## WEEK 5- DAY 5

5 things that occurred today, for which I am thankful:

1 -

2 -

3 -

4 -

5 -

10 things for which I am genuinely grateful in general:

1 -

2 -

3 -

4 -

5 -

6 -

7 -

8 -

9 -

10 -

3 times I noticed the absence of gratitude

1 -

2 -

3 -

How my personal gratitude practice went today:

Lapses and patterns of forgetting:

## WEEK 5- DAY 6

5 things that occurred today, for which I am thankful:
1 -

2 -

3 -

4 -

5 -

10 things for which I am genuinely grateful in general:
1 -

2 -

3 -

4 -

5 -

6 -

7 -

8 -

9 -

10 -

3 times I noticed the absence of gratitude

1 -

2 -

3 -

How my personal gratitude practice went today:

Lapses and patterns of forgetting:

## WEEK 5- DAY 7

5 things that occurred today, for which I am thankful:

1 -

2 -

3 -

4 -

5 -

10 things for which I am genuinely grateful in general:

1 -

2 -

3 -

4 -

5 -

6 -

7 -

8 -

9 -

10 -

3 times I noticed the absence of gratitude

1 -

2 -

3 -

How my personal gratitude practice went today:

Lapses and patterns of forgetting:

Week 5 is now complete. We begin Week 6.

# GRATITUDE PROGRAM - WEEK 6

## A LIFE TRANSFORMED BY GRATITUDE

*I would maintain that thanks are the highest form of thought; and that gratitude is happiness doubled by wonder.*
–G.K. Chesterton

We're told that it takes from three to six months for any change in behavior to become permanent in a person's life.

This week, be thankful all the time - for no reason other than because it is your true character.

Use your journal and be disciplined in your personal gratitude practice.

Commit to gratitude as a key tool for transforming your life. You are transitioning from survival mode to thriving so you can assist in creating a better world.

# WEEK 6- DAY 1

5 things that occurred today, for which I am thankful:

1 -

2 -

3 -

4 -

5 -

10 things for which I am genuinely grateful in general:

1 -

2 -

3 -

4 -

5 -

6 -

7 -

8 -

9 -

10 -

3 times I noticed the absence of gratitude

1 -

2 -

3 -

My personal gratitude practice:

How my gratitude benefits the world:

## WEEK 6- DAY 2

5 things that occurred today, for which I am thankful:

1 -

2 -

3 -

4 -

5 -

10 things for which I am genuinely grateful in general:

1 -

2 -

3 -

4 -

5 -

6 -

7 -

8 -

9 -

10 -

3 times I noticed the absence of gratitude

1 -

2 -

3 -

My personal gratitude practice:

How my gratitude benefits the world:

## WEEK 6- DAY 3

5 things that occurred today, for which I am thankful:

1 -

2 -

3 -

4 -

5 -

10 things for which I am genuinely grateful in general:

1 -

2 -

3 -

4 -

5 -

6 -

7 -

8 -

9 -

10 -

3 times I noticed the absence of gratitude

1 -

2 -

3 -

My personal gratitude practice:

How my gratitude benefits the world:

## WEEK 6- DAY 4

5 things that occurred today, for which I am thankful:

1 -

2 -

3 -

4 -

5 -

10 things for which I am genuinely grateful in general:

1 -

2 -

3 -

4 -

5 -

6 -

7 -

8 -

9 -

10 -

3 times I noticed the absence of gratitude

1 -


2 -


3 -


My personal gratitude practice:

Rich Kenny

# How my gratitude benefits the world:

## WEEK 6- DAY 5

5 things that occurred today, for which I am thankful:

1 -

2 -

3 -

4 -

5 -

10 things for which I am genuinely grateful in general:

1 -

2 -

3 -

4 -

5 -

6 -

7 -

8 -

9 -

10 -

3 times I noticed the absence of gratitude

1 -

2 -

3 -

My personal gratitude practice:

How my gratitude benefits the world:

## WEEK 6- DAY 6

5 things that occurred today, for which I am thankful:

1 -

2 -

3 -

4 -

5 -

10 things for which I am genuinely grateful in general:

1 -

2 -

3 -

4 -

5 -

6 -

7 -

8 -

9 -

10 -

3 times I noticed the absence of gratitude

1 -


2 -


3 -


My personal gratitude practice:

How my gratitude benefits the world:

## WEEK 6- DAY 7

5 things that occurred today, for which I am thankful:

1 -

2 -

3 -

4 -

5 -

10 things for which I am genuinely grateful in general:

1 -

2 -

3 -

4 -

5 -

6 -

7 -

8 -

9 -

10 -

3 times I noticed the absence of gratitude

1 -

2 -

3 -

My personal gratitude practice:

How my gratitude benefits the world:

Week 6 Completes the formal Gratitude Program.

Now the responsibility for keeping gratitude thriving is entirely yours.

The six weeks of the program have helped you to condition your consciousness to gratitude. You have the tools and the experience. You now have an awareness of the tone of gratitude. It will help you as long as you do not neglect it. At times the help will be that gratitude becomes conspicuous by its absence. When that occurs you are equipped to right your own course.

Carry on in gratitude. Welcome to the force that is providing a new and better way for mankind.

Gratitude is the best attitude

# APPRECIATION

I am sincerely and deeply grateful for the love, support and encouragement from my family and friends. They all know of my active commitment to the field of gratitude.

Special thanks to my wife, Mary Ann, for her keen eye and tireless proofreading and exceptional artistry in layout and cover design. She has recently published her own book, Moonchild: A Celebration of Menstruation. It is a unique and valuable work exploring a girl's relationship with menstruation. Visit: https://www.createspace.com/3707055

Photos of the wonders of the natural world are by the author.

Made in the USA
Charleston, SC
24 May 2012